WHO'S THE GOAT?

USING MATH TO CROWN THE CHAMPION™

LEBRON VS DURANT VS CURRY VS JORDAN

David Aretha

rosen publishing's
rosen central®
New York

Published in 2020 by The Rosen Publishing Group, Inc.
29 East 21st Street, New York, NY 10010

First Edition

Library of Congress Cataloging-in-Publication Data

Names: Aretha, David author.
Title: LeBron vs. Durant vs. Curry vs. Jordan / David Aretha.
Other titles: LeBron versus Durant versus Curry versus Jordan
Description: First Edition. | New York : Rosen Publishing, 2020. | Series: Who's the GOAT? Using math to crown the champion | Includes bibliographical references and index. | Audience: Grade 5 to 8.
Identifiers: LCCN 2019005869| ISBN 9781725348479 (library bound) | ISBN 9781725348462 (paperback)
Subjects: LCSH: Basketball players—Rating of—United States—Juvenile literature. | Jordan, Michael, 1963– —Juvenile literature. | James, LeBron—Juvenile literature. | Curry, Stephen, 1988– —Juvenile literature. | Durant, Kevin, 1988– —Juvenile literature. | Basketball players—United States—Statistics. | Basketball—Mathematics—Juvenile literature.
Classification: LCC GV884.A1 A688 2020 | DDC 796.3230922 [B]—dc23
LC record available at https://lccn.loc.gov/2019005869

Manufactured in the United States of America

CONTENTS

INTRODUCTION

LeBron James has won multiple National Basketball Association (NBA) championships and NBA MVP (most valuable player) Awards. He has been voted to fourteen All-Star Games and earned hundreds of millions of dollars. Countless factors motivate James to continue playing at a high level, but among the most important is the Chicago-based ghost of another all-time great: Michael Jordan.

In the 1980s, Michael "Air" Jordan soared and scored like no player in basketball history. He has the highest career scoring average in NBA history at 30.1 points per game (PPG). He led the Chicago Bulls to six NBA Finals and won all of them. He earned the NBA Finals MVP Award all six times.

LeBron's career scoring average hovers around 27 PPG—less than Jordan's. Yet "King" James is a bigger, more powerful player. Through 2018, he had taken his team to the NBA Finals for eight consecutive years, winning three championships in that time. The opponents he faces are taller, stronger, and quicker than those in Jordan's day. Are they better? That is open to debate, as is the question that fans are always chatting about: Is LeBron better than Jordan? Is King James now the GOAT—greatest of all time?

In recent years, two more players have joined the GOAT discussion: Golden State Warriors teammates Stephen Curry and Kevin Durant. Once considered too small to play college basketball, Curry compensated by becoming the greatest shooter ever to set foot on the court, and the numbers prove it. Durant also ranks among history's premier shooters. Like James, he, too, has averaged around 27 PPG in his career. In his day, Jordan never faced a 6-foot-10-inch (208-centimeter) player with the athleticism and feathery shooting touch of KD.

Until 2000, Jordan reigned nearly undisputed as the top basketball player ever. In fact, ESPN ranked His Airness as the greatest athlete of the twentieth century. Wilt Chamberlain, another NBA legend, ranked thirteenth on that same list. Wilt "the Stilt" also averaged 30 PPG for his career, though at 7 feet 1 inch (216 cm) tall, he could easily dominate the shorter, slower centers of his day. Kareem Abdul-Jabbar scored the most points in NBA history (38,387), though his scoring average was 24.6 points per game. In short, Jordan is the greatest of the old legends. James, Curry, and Durant—the three biggest superstars in the modern game—are challenging to become the GOAT.

The NBA is often considered a statistics-heavy league, with analysts able to predict points, rebounds, and other outcomes with relative accuracy based on past results. The players in the GOAT discussion, of course, have the stats to back up their lofty aspirations, and their greatness extends beyond just raw numbers. By combining averages, percentages, and other basic records, all of these players have also posted elite advanced stats that require additional calculation. Those calculations are important because finding an answer to the GOAT question is far from a simple task.

All statistic information is taken from sports-reference .com unless otherwise noted.

CHAPTER 1

AIR JORDAN

From 1983 to 1993, Magic Johnson (left), Michael Jordan (center), and Larry Bird (right) each won three NBA MVP Awards. Their talents helped popularize the game.

By October 29, 1984—in just his third NBA game—Michael Jordan had whipped the city of Chicago into a frenzy. The rookie exhibited so much talent that Bulls fans believed he would lead them to their first-ever NBA championship. On this magical night at Chicago Stadium—known as the Madhouse on Madison Street—Jordan erupted for 37 points against Milwaukee. He not only knew how to score points, he was also already an expert at getting the crowd hyped up. Rather than relying on easy two-pointers, he soared through the air to demonstrate his trademark dunk.

In the 1980s, the NBA's popularity skyrocketed thanks to emerging superstars Magic Johnson, Larry Bird, and—

especially—Michael Jordan. In December 1984, still in his rookie season, MJ appeared on the cover of *Sports Illustrated*. He had already become the new face of the NBA.

Jordan advanced his legend at the 1985 NBA Slam Dunk Contest. On one jam, he took off from the free-throw line and dunked. The effort earned a combined score of fifty from the judges—a perfect ten from each.

How could he jump so high? Maybe his shoes made the difference. By the fall of 1986, Nike had already sold $100 million worth of Air Jordan sneakers. Magic Johnson once humorously described Jordan's leaping ability: "Once Michael gets up there, he says, 'Well, maybe I'll just hang up here in the air for a while, just sit back.' Then all of a sudden, he says, 'Well, maybe I'll 360. No, I changed my mind. I'll go up on the other side.' He's just incredible." His ability to "float" as he jumped up to dunk became his trademark characteristic.

RISE (AND RISE AND RISE ...) TO STARDOM

Born in 1963, Michael Jeffrey Jordan grew up in Wilmington, North Carolina. Both of his parents worked, and together they raised five children. As a sophomore at Laney High School, Michael tried out for the varsity team but did not make it. He used the snub as personal motivation.

Working relentlessly, Michael starred on varsity as a junior and earned All-American honors as a senior. That season, he averaged 26.8 points per game (PPG). To determine his PPG, divide his total points for the season by the total number of games:

$617 \div 23 = 26.8$

After graduation, Jordan attended the University of North Carolina. As a freshman in 1982, he hit the game-winning jump shot in the national championship game. The next two years, he earned first team All-American honors. While in college, MJ took his jump shot to a new level. He would jump high into the air, seem to hang there, then shoot. His sweet shooting and blasts to the rim helped him score on the majority of his attempts. As a junior in 1984, he recorded a field goal

While playing for North Carolina, Jordan established himself as an elite NBA prospect.

percentage of .551. Field goal percentage is calculated by dividing a player's made field goals by their number of attempts. For Jordan:

247 ÷ 448 = .551

With the third pick in the 1984 NBA draft, the Chicago Bulls selected the 6-foot-6-inch (198 cm) jumping-jack out of North Carolina. MJ averaged 28.2 PPG (2,312 ÷ 82 = 28.2) as a rookie, then missed most of his second season (1985–1986) with an injury. In a playoff game against Boston in his 1986 return season, he scored 63 points. In the 1986–1987 season, Jordan averaged a league-leading 37.1 PPG (3,041 ÷ 82 = 37.1). In fact, he averaged almost one point for every minute he played. Points per minute played can be calculated by dividing a player's total points by their total minutes played. For Jordan:

3,041 ÷ 3,281 = 0.93

Overall, Jordan would lead the NBA in PPG ten times. In eight of those seasons, he topped 30 PPG, including 35.0 in 1987–1988 (2,870 ÷ 82 = 35.0).

More than anything, Jordan wanted to deliver an NBA title to Chicago. Unfortunately, the Detroit Pistons eliminated the Bulls from the playoffs in 1988, 1989, and 1990. The Detroit Bad Boys played a rugged defense that physically punished Jordan and his talented teammates,

THE DREAM TEAM

Chuck Daly once described his Dream Team this way: "It was like Elvis and the Beatles put together."

When it comes to teams, the 1992 US Olympic basketball squad was the undeniable GOAT. The team featured Magic Johnson and Michael Jordan in the backcourt and legends Larry Bird and Karl Malone at forward. All-time greats David Robinson and Patrick Ewing split time at center, while John Stockton—the NBA career assist leader—backed up Magic at point guard. On top of all that, Hall of Famers Charles Barkley, Clyde Drexler, Chris Mullin, and Scottie Pippen were ready to come off the bench.

Chuck Daly, the dapperly dressed coach of the Detroit Pistons, had the privilege of coaching this "Dream Team." The 1992 Summer Olympics, in Barcelona, Spain, allowed professional basketball players to participate for the first time—so Team USA Basketball loaded up the roster with the NBA's best, plus forward Christian Laettner of Duke University. The US team opened with a 116-48 demolition of Angola—their biggest blowout of the eight-game tournament. Their closest match came in the gold-medal game, when they defeated Croatia, 117-85. Jordan averaged a solid 14.9 PPG for the tournament.

including future Hall of Famer Scottie Pippen. The Pistons implemented a unique set of strategies to contain MJ—but Jordan worked tirelessly to overcome the challenge.

In 1991, the Bulls swept the Pistons in four games in the Eastern Conference Finals. The Bad Boys pouted, walking off the court in Game 4 before the final buzzer had sounded. Jordan then led Chicago to a five-game triumph over Magic Johnson's Lakers in the NBA Finals. In the victorious Bulls locker room, MJ hugged the

Sneakers were just sneakers until MJ's signature Air Jordans became all the rage in the 1980s.

championship trophy and cried. In the five games of the championship series, MJ scored 156 points, for a strong Finals average of 31.2 PPG (156 ÷ 5 = 31.2).

In the 1991–1992 and 1992–1993 seasons, Jordan again led the Bulls to NBA titles. First, they shut down the Portland Trail Blazers in the NBA Finals, then they blotted out the Phoenix Suns. By this point, Jordan reigned as the most famous athlete in the world. Kids—from Mexico to Brazil to China—were wearing Jordan jerseys. In addition to buying Air Jordan sneakers, kids wore baggy shorts like Jordan's. Some wore hoop earrings and even shaved their heads bald—just to be "like Mike."

THREE MORE TITLES—AND THREE RETIREMENTS

In October 1993, Jordan shocked the world when he announced his retirement from basketball at age thirty. He wanted to pursue a whole new challenge: professional baseball, a sport he had enjoyed as a youth. He played the 1994 season in the Chicago White Sox's minor league system as a member of the Birmingham Barons. Minor league teams travel to away games on buses, and Jordan bought the Barons a deluxe bus so they could travel in style. Unfortunately for baseball fans, MJ's basketball skills did not transfer well to the sport, and after a single season, he returned to the Bulls in 1995.

Along with Jordan and Pippen, the 1995–1996 Bulls featured master rebounder Dennis Rodman, who adorned his body with tattoos and piercings and dyed his hair a variety of rainbow colors. He stood in stark contrast to the coach of the Bulls' dynasty: tall, calm, bearded, and cerebral Phil Jackson. Together, the 1995–1996 Bulls won a then-record seventy-two games. This put their winning percentage at an unbelievable .878. Winning percentage is calculated by dividing a team's total victories by the total number of games it played:

$$72 \div 82 = .878$$

The Bulls slowed down the Seattle SuperSonics and emerged victorious in the 1996 NBA Finals. In the 1997 NBA Finals, the Bulls and the Utah Jazz entered Game 5 tied at two victories each. Prior to the game, Jordan was so sick that he could barely get out of bed. Showing the will of a champion, he played in the game and scored 38 points en route to a 90–88 victory for the Bulls—after which he collapsed into Pippen's arms. "Probably the most difficult thing I've ever done," Jordan said after the game. "I almost played myself into passing out just to win a basketball game."

One year later, in his last game ever for Chicago, MJ hit one of the biggest shots in NBA history. The Bulls led Utah three games to two in the NBA Finals, but the Jazz led Game 6 at 86–85 with eight seconds left. With

The legendary Jordan and multitalented forward Scottie Pippen (right) powered the Chicago Bulls to a total of six NBA championships.

almost no time remaining, Jordan drove into the lane, stopped instantly, and pulled up for an 18-foot (5.5-meter) jumper to put the Bulls on top.

Jordan retired from basketball for three years following the 1997–1998 season. Then, at age thirty-eight, he returned to play two seasons with the Washington Wizards. He retired permanently in 2003 with a career scoring average of 30.12 PPG (32,292 ÷ 1,072 = 30.1). That remains the NBA record, with no modern players even coming close to breaking it.

CHAPTER 2

KING JAMES

When he awoke on Christmas morning 1987 in Akron, Ohio, LeBron James did not understand the drama that was enveloping his life. All he knew was that he got to open presents. A week earlier, Michael Jordan—his future hero—had scored 52 points against the Cleveland Cavaliers. That morning, three-year-old LeBron unwrapped a plastic basketball hoop. Just hours earlier, his beloved grandma, Freda James, had died of a heart attack.

STRUGGLES TO SUCCESS

LeBron's mother, Gloria James, worried about her future and that of her son. Having given birth to her only child at age sixteen, she had relied on the big old house and full-time paycheck her mother had provided. After her mother's death, Gloria worked a variety of jobs but could not afford to maintain the house. From age five to eight, LeBron moved a dozen times with his mother. Most troubling to LeBron, he often spent days without seeing her. One of his greatest fears was losing her like he had his grandmother.

Eventually, Gloria secured a long-term apartment and LeBron's life stabilized. Big and athletic, he dominated in football and basketball. From age eleven to fourteen, he traveled the country with the Northeast Ohio Shooting Stars, an Amateur Athletic Union team. At Saint Vincent-Saint Mary (SVSM) High School in Akron, he became the most talked-about high school basketball player of all time.

Though Michael Jordan had failed to make varsity as a sophomore, James dominated varsity competition when he was still a freshman. He led SVSM to a 27–0 record and a state championship. In twenty-seven games, he scored 487 points for an 18.0 PPG (487 ÷ 27 = 18.0) average. He excelled in all phases—not just shooting—averaging 6.2 rebounds, 3.6 assists, and 3.1 steals per game. These averages are found by dividing his overall numbers by the total number of games played:

168 rebounds ÷ 27 games = 6.2 rebounds per game (RPG)
96 assists ÷ 27 games = 3.6 assists per game (APG)
84 steals ÷ 27 games = 3.1 steals per game (SPG)

As he developed into a 6-foot-8-inch (203 cm), 240-pound (109 kilogram) powerhouse, James's high school feats stunned the nation. He led the SVSM Fighting

As a freshman, LeBron led SVSM to a 27-0 record and the state title. As a junior, he was National Player of the Year.

Irish to four state title games and three championships. He became the first sophomore ever named first team All-American by *USA Today*. The next year, he was named *USA Today*'s National Player of the Year—the first junior to earn that honor. As a senior, he averaged 30.4 PPG (730 ÷ 24 = 30.4).

THE KING OF CLEVELAND

Akron is located just south of Cleveland, Ohio, and in May 2003, fans in Northeast Ohio were excited when the Cavaliers won the NBA draft lottery. The Cavs—a team that had never won an NBA title—got to draft first overall that spring.

With James, the Cavs improved from seventeen wins in the 2002–2003 season to thirty-five in his rookie year. They still had a losing record, though, at 35–47, for a winning percentage of just .427 (35 ÷ 82 = .427).

The immensely strong King James could rumble to the basket, score on power moves around the rim, shoot midrange jump shots, and pass the ball like a guard. Cleveland fans adored him, especially when he began every game by tossing powder into the air, making a magical appearance on the court. As NBA Rookie of the Year in the 2003–2004 season, he averaged 20.9 PPG (1,651 ÷ 79 = 20.9). His maturity at just nineteen years old was also incredibly impressive.

The next year, James was selected to play in the NBA All-Star Game—for the first of fifteen consecutive seasons. He also averaged 27.2 PPG (2,176 ÷ 80 = 27.2), 7.4 RPG (592 ÷ 80 = 7.4), and 7.2 APG (576 ÷ 80 = 7.2) that year, numbers that would become typical of every season of his career. He also recorded his first career triple-double. A game recorded as a triple-double means double figures (ten or more) in points, rebounds,

With his explosive quickness and powerful frame, LeBron was an unstoppable force on drives to the rim, even against older players.

and assists in a game. He also led the NBA in minutes per game (MPG), with 42.4. MPG can be calculated by dividing a player's total number of minutes played by the number of games played in a season. For James:

$3{,}392 \div 80 = 42.4$

In the spring of 2007, after several more individually strong seasons, James led the Cavaliers to the NBA Finals, where they lost to Kobe Bryant and the Los Angeles Lakers. James won the NBA scoring title in 2007–2008, with 30.0 PPG ($2{,}250 \div 75 = 30.0$), and claimed the NBA MVP Award the following two years. He was making a case for himself as one of the NBA's brightest stars—and maybe even capable of matching the greatness of MJ.

James did everything except achieve his ultimate goal: bringing a championship to Cleveland. Before the 2010–2011 season, he did the unimaginable: he left. As a free agent in 2010, he signed with the Miami Heat.

BOX PLUS/MINUS

Though he has never set foot on the court as a player, Daniel Myers has contributed a lot to professional basketball. This mathematician created an important statistic called box plus/minus (BPM). A complex calculation with many variables, BPM reveals how much value a player brings to his team when he is on the court. An NBA All-Star-level player will earn a score of around +5. In short, that means he is worth an additional 5 points to his team for every 100 possessions that the team has. An average NBA player would have a rating of 0.

BPM is a great way to measure James's value to his team. Besides scoring around 27 PPG, he often runs the offense. He analyzes the defense and gets the ball to the teammates who are in the best position to score. He also attracts double-teams, meaning his four other teammates face just three defenders. Importantly, he also excels as a rebounder and defender.

Statisticians have rated NBA players in BPM dating back to 1973. Michael Jordan led the NBA in the stat for four straight seasons, with a record high of +12.56 in 1988–1989. Beginning in 2007–2008, LeBron led the league in BPM for seven straight years, including a record-breaking +12.99 in the 2008–2009 season.

Cavs fans, executives, and analysts were both shocked and offended by this move. Most viewed it as a betrayal. Some called him a coward or a traitor and were angry that he was willing to throw his hometown team away.

These were harsh reactions to the decision of a player who had given his heart and soul to the Cavaliers. Among his many charitable contributions, the big-hearted James has donated millions of dollars to provide hundreds of scholarships to underprivileged children in Akron. In part to escape the enormous pressures he faced in Cleveland, he made the move to Miami.

BATTLING FOR CHAMPIONSHIPS

In four seasons with Miami, James won two more NBA MVP Awards. He and superstar guard Dwyane Wade led the Heat to four Eastern Conference titles and two NBA championships. They defeated Kevin Durant and Oklahoma City in the 2012 NBA Finals and Tim Duncan and San Antonio in the following year's Finals. The only thing missing from James's incredible career performances in Cleveland were NBA titles, and with the Heat, he finally had the rings to back up his play.

After four years with the Heat, something amazing happened; a free agent in summer 2014, James announced on *Sports Illustrated*'s website: "I'm coming home." Across Cleveland, fans rejoiced at the news, honking horns and high-fiving strangers in the streets. In four more seasons with Cleveland (before eventually signing with the Lakers in 2018), James carried the Cavs to four appearances in the NBA Finals, each time facing

Cavaliers fans were angry and heartbroken when James signed with Miami in 2010—but they joyously celebrated his return to the team in 2014.

off against Stephen Curry and the Golden State Warriors. Widely hailed as the greatest NBA team of all time, the Warriors won three of the four battles.

In 2016, however, the Cavs overcame a 3–1 deficit to defeat Golden State, and James won the Finals MVP Award. Throughout the 2016 Finals, the Cavs averaged 100.4 points (703 ÷ 7 = 100.4), 43.9 rebounds (307 ÷ 7 = 43.9), and 18.0 assists (126 ÷ 7 = 18) per game. James himself averaged 29.7 PPG (208 ÷ 7 = 29.7), 11.3 RPG (79 ÷ 7 = 11.3), and 8.9 APG

(62 ÷ 7 = 8.9). What percentage of the team's total offense did James produce? To calculate this, divide his personal contribution by the total team statistic:

29.7 individual PPG ÷ 100.4 team PPG = .296 (29.6 percent)
11.3 individual RPG ÷ 43.9 team RPG = .257 (25.7 percent)

In 2016—for the first time in the team's forty-six-year history—the Cleveland Cavaliers won the NBA title. LeBron could not hold back his tears.

8.9 individual APG ÷ 18.0 team APG = .494 (49.4 percent)

Because these calculations result in a percentage, move the decimal point two places to the right to find the converted percent. James's numbers during the Finals were remarkable. Fourteen total players recorded statistics for the Cavs, which means—on average—any single player should be contributing 7.1 percent to any statistic (100 ÷ 14 = 7.1). Accordingly, James was roughly 4 times as valuable in scoring points (29.6 ÷ 7.1 = 4.1), 3.6 times more valuable for rebounds (25.7 ÷ 7.1 = 3.6), and nearly 7 times as valuable in recording assists (49.4 ÷ 7.1 = 6.9). At the end of the seven-game series—after single-handedly carrying his team to victory—James crouched facedown on the court, overcome with emotion. He had finally delivered a title to Cleveland.

CHAPTER 3

CHEF CURRY

Long before Stephen Curry transformed the Golden State Warriors into annual NBA title contenders, America fell in love with him. As an adorable tyke, little Steph appeared in a Burger King commercial with his father, NBA sharpshooter Dell Curry. While walking around their neighborhood, Dell says in the ad, "Stephen, what do you want to be when you grow up?"

"A basketball player," Stephen responds immediately.

"Boy, that's gonna take a lot of hard work and practice," Dell says. "You gotta study hard too."

"I know!"

DON'T TELL HIM THE ODDS

The odds of a young Curry making it to the NBA were astronomical. A maximum of 450 men can play in the league at any given time, and around 3.8 billion men inhabit the world. Divide that huge number by 450, and the answer is Curry's chance of playing in the NBA: 1 in 84 million.

In seven straight seasons with the Charlotte Hornets, Dell Curry shot over .400 from three-point range; he passed that accuracy down to Steph.

Yet Steph inherited his father's shooting touch. With Milwaukee in 1998–1999, Dell led the NBA in three-point shooting at .476. The percentage for three-point shooting—an important part of Steph's game—is calculated by dividing a player's number of completed three-point attempts by their total three-point attempts. For Dell in 1998–1999:

69 ÷ 145 = .476

Despite a successful high school career, universities with strong basketball programs passed on Steph because they thought he was too small. The 6-foot-1-inch (185 cm), 160-pounder (72.5 kg) went to tiny Davidson College outside Charlotte, North Carolina. Working extra hard on his shooting form, Steph averaged 21.5 PPG (731 ÷ 34 = 21.5) in 2006–2007. Among the nation's freshmen that season, only Kevin Durant scored more. As a sophomore, Curry averaged 25.9 PPG (932 ÷ 36 = 25.9) and ranked second in the country with

When he left Davidson College, Curry ranked fourth in NCAA history with 414 career three-pointers—and he played just three seasons at the school.

4.5 three-pointers per game. To calculate a player's three-point attempts per game, divide their total number of attempts by their number of games played. For Curry:

162 ÷ 36 = 4.5

In that spring's NCAA (National Collegiate Athletic Association) tournament, he scored 40 and 30 points in the first two games, respectively, to stunningly send Davidson to the top sixteen. LeBron James himself showed up for Davidson's next game against Wisconsin, impressed by what he had heard about the budding star. Davidson defeated Wisconsin before falling to powerhouse Kansas.

As a first team All-American in 2008–2009, Curry led the nation in scoring with 28.6 PPG (972 ÷ 34 = 28.6). In the 2009 NBA draft, the Golden State Warriors selected him with the seventh overall pick. Curry was then headed to Oakland, California.

SHOOTING STAR

In his first five seasons with the Warriors, Curry averaged 20.3 PPG (6,821 ÷ 336 = 20.3). From the three-point arc, he shot a remarkable .440 over those five years. Though undersized at 6 feet 3 inches (190.5 cm), it did not matter—because Curry shot the ball before defenders could get in his face. ESPN's Sport Science reported that Steph's release time was a speedy 0.4 seconds. That figure covers the amount of time it took for him to begin his shot and release the ball—quite a lot to do in .4 seconds.

Curry also had near-perfect shooting mechanics, including the arc he created on his shot. Shooters do not want to fire a line-drive shot (meaning one with a low arc) because the ball would approach the hoop flat; so it likely would bang off the front or back rim. A rainbow shot (meaning one with a high, defined arc) would not work either—the higher the ball rises, the harder it is to control its accuracy. The ideal arc on a shot is in the middle, at around 45 degrees. Working with the *Wall Street Journal*, physicist Eric Goff analyzed Curry's three-pointers. He found that they entered the rim at around 46 degrees—practically perfect.

Each season, Curry has taken his game to a new level. In 2012–2013, he led the NBA in three-pointers made (272)—the first of five straight seasons he would do so. The next season, he made the All-Star team for

Steph's lightning-quick release and smart angles allow him to get shots off before defenders can get in his face.

the first time. In the 2014–2015 season, he riddled opponents with threes from relatively extreme distances. In one game against Dallas, he nailed ten threes and totaled 51 points. In addition to a quick release and an advantageous angle, he was shooting the ball from so far away that it was impossible to defend. Curry and his "Splash Brother" teammate Klay Thompson led the Warriors to a 67–15 record, with Chef Curry cooking up his first NBA MVP title.

STEPH CURRY VS. STEVE KERR

By the end of the 2015–2016 season, Stephen Curry owned the second-highest career three-point percentage in NBA history: .444. Curry did not have to go far to find the top-ranked guy on the all-time list. It was Steve Kerr, the head coach of the Warriors. Kerr made 725 three-pointers in 1,599 attempts, making his three-point percentage .454 (725 ÷ 1,599 = .454).

Kerr, however, will be the first to admit that he was not a better shooter than Curry. Why? There are several factors. First, for part of Kerr's career (1994–1997), the three-point arc was only 22 feet (6.7 m) from the basket. Kerr took advantage by shooting nearly .498 on threes for those years. Since 1997, the arc has been 23.75 feet (7.2 m) from the rim.

Second, the game was played at a slightly slower speed during Kerr's career. He had a bit more time to set up and release his three-pointers. Curry, meanwhile, catches and releases almost instantaneously.

Third, Kerr teamed up for four seasons with Michael Jordan—it is no coincidence that these were Kerr's most productive three-point seasons. MJ attracted double-teams and triple-teams, leaving Kerr wide open at the arc. Curry has not had that luxury. With Golden State, Curry is the one who has attracted the double-teams. Even with opponents constantly in his face, he still buries the bombs.

In the 2015 playoffs, Curry swished ninety-eight three-pointers, breaking the NBA single-season playoff record by a shocking forty completions. As the Warriors smashed New Orleans, Memphis, and then Houston to reach the NBA Finals, the roar inside Golden State's Oracle Arena was deafening. Golden State then defeated Cleveland and LeBron James in six games in the NBA Finals. Oakland celebrated their first NBA championship in forty years. During the victory parade on a spectacularly sunny day, Steph Curry stood atop a double-decker Warriors bus with one arm around his wife, Ayesha, and his other arm around the championship trophy. All the while, blue and gold confetti rained from the sky.

SO MANY THREES

In 2015–2016, the Warriors elevated their overall game to a new level. They ran at a fast pace, whipped the ball around, and fired shots with lightning quickness. The Dubs, as they are known, began the season at 24–0, the greatest start in NBA history, and finished with the best record the league has ever seen: 73–9. Curry led the league with 30.1 PPG (2,378 ÷ 79 = 30.1) and sank 402 three-pointers, breaking his own NBA record of 286. He broke the record by an astonishing 40.6 percent: 402 – 286 = 116; 116 ÷ 286 = .406. Following the season, Curry became the first unanimous MVP in NBA history; all 131 voters selected him.

Curry and his Warriors teammates are shown here receiving their rings for winning the 2018 NBA championship; it was the team's third title in four years.

The Warriors seemed headed to their second straight championship, leading Cleveland in the NBA Finals three games to one. However, LeBron James led an all-time great comeback to secure the Cavaliers' first-ever NBA title. After that season, the Warriors signed superstar free agent Kevin Durant. Golden State breezed to NBA crowns in both 2017 and 2018, defeating LeBron and the Cavs each time.

The success of Curry and the Warriors has changed the NBA. Flinging the ball around and launching threes has become the latest strategic fad. NBA teams averaged 7.8 made three-pointers per game in 2014–2015. That number steadily increased to 10.5 in 2017–2018. That is a 35 percent increase (10.5 – 7.8 = 2.7; 2.7 ÷ 7.8 = .35). In 2016, *Sports Illustrated* reported that kids across the nation had contracted "Stephitis"—the drive to launch three-point shots. Most significantly, Curry showed that even small players—by basketball standards—can reach the game's pinnacle.

CHAPTER 4

KEVIN DURANT, THE SLIM REAPER

Tough love: those words characterize how Wanda Durant raised her two sons, largely by herself. She knew that as young, black males in Washington, D.C., her boys faced difficult challenges. Many of Washington's black males drop out of high school and can wind up in jail, prison, or morgues.

When a young Kevin told Wanda he wanted to play in the NBA when he got older, she told him she would allow it—but he would have to prove his dedication. He did, training daily with a coach who worked him hard. Conditioning included endless running, crab walks, duck walks, and—worst of all—climbing the hill outside the gym. The hill rose 50 yards (45.7 m) high at a steep incline. One trip up could be exhausting; Durant's coach would make him climb it dozens of times in a row.

As serious as his coach was, his mother was even tougher. Kevin acknowledged his mother's influence and love during his NBA MVP Award acceptance speech in 2014. Through heavy tears, he looked her in the eyes and said, "You're the real MVP."

Durant was incredible at the University of Texas. He could dominate inside like a center and swish jumpers like a shooting guard.

BRINGING THE THUNDER

As a physical specimen, Kevin Durant has it all going for him. He was gifted with a 6-foot-10-inch (208 cm) body, unbelievable coordination, and enormous athleticism. Moreover, since childhood, he has owned a stunningly accurate shooting touch. With a calm, methodical approach to improvement—and countless hours of work in the gym—he has developed into one of the all-time greats.

At the University of Texas in 2007, Durant became the first freshman to win a national player of the year award. In fact, he won all seven such awards that year, including the Wooden Award and Naismith College Player of the Year Award. He averaged 25.8 PPG ($903 \div 35 = 25.8$) and 11.1 RPG ($389 \div 35 = 11.1$). As a comparison, Michael Jordan averaged 13.5 PPG ($459 \div 34 = 13.5$) as a college freshman.

In 2007, the Seattle SuperSonics selected Durant with the second overall pick in the NBA draft. The Sonics won just nineteen games in the 2007–2008 season, but Kevin averaged 20.3 PPG (1,625 ÷ 80 = 20.3)—tops on the team. One year later, the Sonics moved to Oklahoma City and were renamed the Thunder. The state of Oklahoma, which had never had a major professional sports team, embraced Durant immediately. Similarly, KD found Oklahoma City a nice place to settle in. "It's very slowed down here," he told Rick Maese of the *Washington Post*. "I like it that way. I'm a guy that's very reserved, quiet and shy myself."

Durant unleashed thunder in his jams, and he struck like lightning from outside. He averaged 25.3 PPG (1,872 ÷ 74 = 25.3) in the team's first season in Oklahoma. He became the second-youngest player, behind only LeBron James, to average 25 PPG in a season. While Stephen Curry was known as the shooter with swagger on the court, Durant was the quiet "Slim Reaper." He was soft-spoken, kind to everyone, and deeply devoted to his Christian faith. Sometimes, it seemed, the only sound he made was that

Durant led the NBA with an impressive 30.1 points in the 2009–2010 season at the tender age of twenty-one.

of the ball swishing through the nylon. David Ramsey of *The Gazette* portrayed him as "a peaceful jump shooter in a league dominated by howling dunkers. He goes out of his way to blend in with his teammates. He's remarkably tranquil."

POINTS BY THE THOUSANDS

KD broke into the big time in the 2009–2010 season. He made the NBA All-Star Game for the first of many eventual appearances during the decade. He took the Thunder to their first playoff appearance—and he led the league in scoring with 30.1 PPG. He also paced the NBA in both total field goals made (794)—128 of which were three-pointers—and free throws made (756). How many total points did he have in 2009–2010? Calculating total points takes multiple steps: 794 total field goals – 128 three-pointers = 666 two-pointers. The 666 two-pointers were worth a total of 1,332 points (666 × 2 = 1,332). His 128 three-pointers totaled 384 points (128 × 3 = 384). His 756 free throws equaled, of course, 756 points. So his total points were 1,332 + 384 + 756 = 2,472. Dividing that total by his number of games produces his PPG average: 2,472 ÷ 82 =30.1.

Durant captured the NBA scoring title in the 2010–2011, 2011–2012, and 2013–2014 seasons. His four scoring crowns tied him with all-time greats George

WIN SHARES

In Major League Baseball, the WAR stat is all the rage. It is a statistical calculation that stands for wins above replacement. In 2018, Mookie Betts of the Boston Red Sox had a Major League-high WAR of 10.9. In other words, he was worth 10.9 more wins to his team than an average player.

The NBA has a lesser-known—but similar—statistic called win shares. This complex calculation divvies up each team's win totals among its players. For example, imagine an NBA team that won fifty games last season. Its coach used ten players during the season, and each player contributed, statistically, an equal amount to the team's success. In such a scenario, each player would have a win share rating of 5 (50 wins ÷ 10 players = 5 win shares).

As of March 2019, the all-time leaders in career win shares are: Kareem Abdul-Jabbar (273), Wilt Chamberlain (247), and Karl Malone (235). This makes sense, as each of these large legends dominated around the rim. Back in the old days, teams would try to feed the ball to their big man for easy baskets. The next two on the list are LeBron James (224) and Michael Jordan (214). Curry and Durant are much farther down, largely because they have not played as many seasons.

Gervin and Allen Iverson for the third most in NBA history. Only Michael Jordan (ten) and Wilt Chamberlain (seven) have won more. In his 2013–2014 MVP season,

Durant set career highs in both PPG (2,592 ÷ 81 = 32.0) and APG (446 ÷ 81 = 5.5). That means he was directly involved in 43 points per contest. An assist resulted in two points for a teammate: 5.5 × 2 = 11. Adding that to his PPG average produces the number of points for which he was responsible for per game: 32 + 11 = 43. There were many reasons for this offensive dominance, starting with his sharpshooting ability. Steph Curry is largely known as a three-point sniper, but KD can put up points from everywhere.

In 2012–2013, Durant joined the exclusive .500-.400.-900 club, meaning he made more than 50 percent of his field goals, shot over .400 from the three-point arc, and eclipsed .900 from the free-throw line. Durant and Curry are among only seven players who have accomplished this in an NBA season ever. Durant and superstar guard Russell Westbrook turned the Thunder into annual title contenders. In 2012, they made it to the NBA Finals, eventually losing to LeBron James and the Miami Heat. They also reached the Western Conference Finals in 2011, 2014, and 2016.

TEAMING UP WITH STEPH

Though the Thunder could not realize their title dreams, Oklahoma City fans still loved Durant. When tornadoes ripped through one of the city's suburbs, KD arrived to lend a hand and donated $1 million to victims. He started a program for children called the Strong and Kind movement. A wrecking ball on the court and a hero in the community, his career was shaping up to be one of the greatest in history.

That said, many Oklahomans turned on Durant when he signed a free agent deal with the Golden State Warriors in July 2016. Similar to Cleveland fans' feelings about LeBron James's departure, fans felt he owed his success to the supporters who had followed his rising star. To make things worse, the Thunder had just lost to

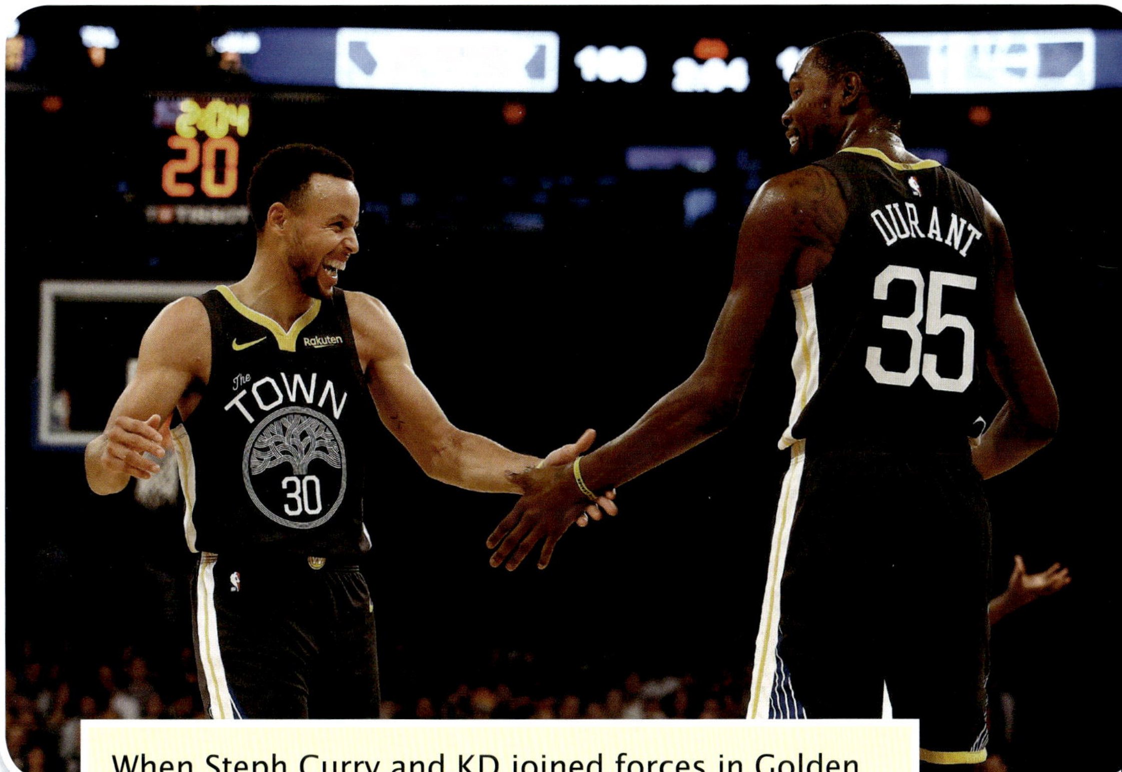

When Steph Curry and KD joined forces in Golden State in 2016–2017, the Warriors became nearly unbeatable. They went 16–1 in the postseason to win the NBA title.

the Warriors in that year's NBA playoffs. There was a lot of bad feeling between the two cities, especially since Durant was the cornerstone of a team that believed it was building for a long, successful future.

The Warriors had won an NBA-record 73 games in 2015–2016. Now they added Durant to the mix. Many fans wondered: would they win every single game? Not quite. The Warriors finished 67–15 in the 2016–2017 season. Remarkably, four of the twelve Western

In his first two seasons with the Warriors, Durant raised two NBA championship trophies and two NBA Finals MVP awards.

Conference All-Stars played for the Warriors: Durant, Curry, fellow three-point bomber Klay Thompson, and forward Draymond Green. With so many offensive weapons, Durant took the fewest shots of his career: 16.5 (1,023 ÷ 62 = 16.5) per game. Yet with so many other players to guard, KD had easier shots, resulting in a career-best .537 field goal percentage (550 ÷ 1,023 = .537). He averaged 25.1 PPG (1,556 ÷ 62 = 25.1).

Golden State breezed to the 2017 NBA title, going 16–1 in the postseason and utterly dominating Cleveland and LeBron James in the NBA Finals. Durant earned the Finals MVP Award, averaging 35.2 PPG (176 ÷ 5 = 35.2) in the five-game series. After all those difficult climbs up the hill as a kid, Durant had reached the top of the NBA mountain. One year later, he and his team did it again. The Warriors swept the Cavs in the championship series, and Durant earned his second NBA Finals MVP Award.

CHAPTER 5

WHO'S THE GOAT?

From Chicago to Miami, from Cleveland to Los Angeles, fans have debated the question for years: Who is better—MJ or King James? What about Curry and Durant? For starters, it is important to investigate who the greatest player of the twenty-first century is. After all, there is little doubt that Jordan is the leader among twentieth-century players, so the greatest player of the current century will have to go head-to-head with MJ if they want to have a claim to the title of GOAT.

THE GREATEST OF THE TWENTY-FIRST CENTURY

The purpose of comparing stats is to take the three top superstars of today and compare them to the greatest legends of the past.

In 2018, *SLAM* produced a list of the 100 top NBA players of all time. Their top ten, in order, were: Michael Jordan, LeBron James, Magic Johnson, Kareem Abdul-Jabbar, Kobe Bryant, Shaquille O'Neal, Bill Russell, Wilt

The star power of Shaquille O'Neal (left) and Kobe Bryant resulted in three straight NBA championships for the Los Angeles Lakers: 2000, 2001, and 2002.

Chamberlain, Tim Duncan, and Larry Bird. *SLAM* listed Durant as thirteenth and Curry nineteenth.

The only twenty-first century players on *SLAM*'s top twenty are: James, Bryant, O'Neal, Durant, and Curry. Based on career totals, it appears that James, Bryant, and O'Neal are better than both Durant and Curry:

Player	Seasons (games played)	Points	Assists	Rebounds	MVP Awards	NBA Finals appearances	NBA titles
LeBron James	15 (1,186)	31,038	8,208	8,415	4	9	3
Kobe Bryant	20 (1,346)	33,643	6,306	7,047	1	7	5
Shaquille O'Neal	19 (1,207)	28,596	3,026	13,099	1	6	4
Kevin Durant	11 (831)	20,913	3,029	5,495	1	3	2
Stephen Curry	9 (675)	14,434	4,227	2,763	2	4	3

When looking at per-game averages, however, it is harder to differentiate between these top-five twenty-first century stars. Per-game averages are calculated by dividing a player's total statistics by the total number of games played in his career. Additional stats in this table are three-pointers per game (3PG), three-point percentage (3PT%), field-goal percentage (FG%), and free-throw percentage (FT%).

Player	PPG	APR	RPG	3PG	3PT%	FG%	FT%
James	27.2	7.2	7.4	1.4	.344	.504	.739
Bryant	25.0	4.7	5.2	1.4	.329	.447	.837
O'Neal	23.7	2.5	10.9	0.0	.045	.582	.527
Durant	27.1	3.9	7.1	1.9	.384	.491	.884
Curry	23.1	6.8	4.4	3.4	.436	.477	.903

In analyzing the per-game stats, James stands out, even among this best-of-the-century list. He boasts the highest PPG and APG of the bunch, and his rebounding average is second best. If KD and Curry play until they hit nineteen or twenty seasons, like Shaq and Bryant, their totals should look just as strong—and it is likely they will win more NBA championships.

Despite the undeniable success of the relatively new stars Curry and Durant, nearly everyone agrees that the two best players of all time are Jordan and James. In addition to *SLAM*, most sports analysis sites, publications, and experts rank these two at the top of the list of all-time greats.

JORDAN VS. JAMES

If the NBA stood for the National Bowling Association, it would be possible to determine if Jordan or James was better based just on their scoring average. In basketball, however, scoring does not fully define a player—though it is a good start.

At the conclusion of the 2017–2018 season, James had a career scoring average of 27.2 PPG, fourth best of all time. Jordan holds the number-one spot, with 30.1 PPG. MJ has averaged 2.9 more PPG than James (30.1 – 27.2 = 2.9).

However, other stats are important as well. Statisticians have argued that an assist is equivalent to approximately one point since the passer contributes about equally to the made field goal. It is also reasonable to claim that a rebound is worth about one point, as it can contribute to a team's eventual scoring. Here is how the two players matched up with their career averages:

Player	PPG	APG	RPG
Jordan	30.1	5.3	6.2
James	27.2	7.2	7.4

If each player is given one point for each APG and one point for each RPG, their numbers look like this:

Player	PPG	APG	RPG	Combined points
Jordan	30.1 +	5.3 +	6.2 =	41.6
James	27.2 +	7.2 +	7.4 =	41.8

Looking at these combined points averages, it is clear that His Airness and King James are both equally royal in their offensive performance. Of course, other stats are important, too. Jordan averaged 2.3 steals per game and 0.8 blocked shots per game. James averaged 1.8 steals and 0.8 blocks per game. The slight edge here goes to MJ.

What about shooting percentages? Here is how they compare:

Player	2PT%	3PT%	FT%
Jordan	.510	.327	.835
James	.504	.344	.739

Here, Jordan gains an advantage because his free-throw percentage is so much higher. Free-throw percentage is significant. Jordan had more than 9,000 attempts in his career, and James will almost certainly reach or surpass that total before his retirement.

In analyzing all the numbers presented so far, it is easy to see why the race is so close between these two elite players. Each has compiled statistics that other players can only dream of, and James has many productive seasons ahead of him. However, there is more to consider.

In comparing PPG of players in different eras, it is necessary to evaluate the league-scoring average of each era. During the seasons that Jordan played, NBA teams averaged 97 PPG. During LeBron's career, teams have averaged 100 PPG. This information is useful for determining what percentage of the average PPG each player was producing. Jordan averaged 30 PPG while NBA teams were averaging 97. To find the percentage Jordan produced, divide his individual PPG by the league average: 30 ÷ 97 = .31 (31 percent). James averaged 27 PPG while NBA teams were averaging 100, so: 27 ÷ 100 = .27 (27 percent). This analysis makes Jordan's scoring look even more impressive—adjusting for the evolution of the league, he was producing points at an unbelievable level.

THE COACHES' POLL

In 2018, CBS Sports polled 100 college coaches anonymously, asking them if they thought Jordan or James was the greatest of all time. Nearly everyone polled picked MJ; only eighteen selected King James. Perhaps they were biased, because members of older generations tend to be nostalgic about MJ. In any event, there were two interesting responses among those polled:

"Not even close—it's Jordan. Because the object of the game is to win ... I'd rather go to

While many coaches prefer the overall talents of Jordan, James is bigger and stronger; he often has to power through multiple defenders to take a clean shot.

a surgeon who's operated six successful heart surgeries and no one dies as opposed to a guy that's failed six times."

"LeBron is bigger, stronger, faster and very skilled. He'd be the best player in the world if he were a center, point guard or anywhere in between. Nobody has ever been that versatile."

It is also worth noting that James has yet to reach the declining phase of his career. As players get older—and slower—their per-game numbers almost always go down. Jordan performed at his peak through 1998. From his rookie season through his last peak season of 1997–1998, he averaged 31.5 PPG. By the end of 2018, James was still at his peak and his PPG was 27.2. So, "peak Jordan" (31.5) was a considerably better scorer than "peak LeBron" (27.2).

There are advanced stats—including BPM and VORP (value over replacement player)—to measure players. VORP, similar to win shares, is a method for calculating how much more useful any given player is than the player's replacement. Jordan owns a career BPM of 8.09 (second best in NBA history), while James ranks first at 9.14. MJ is also second in career VORP at 104.4, while

King James reigns supreme with an enormous total of 127.7. Of course, there are also less complicated ways of measuring a player's greatness, including the following:

Player	Jordan	James
NBA championships	6	3
NBA Finals appearances	6	9
NBA MVP Awards	5	4
All-Star Games	14	15
Scoring titles	10	1
First-team All-NBA	10	12
First-team All-Defensive	9	5
NBA Finals MVP Awards	6	3

FINAL CONSIDERATIONS

In sports, a player's intangible talents cannot be properly measured with numbers. Is the player a vocal leader? Does he lead by example? Does he analyze the defense and make smart decisions with the basketball? Is he a winner? Is he courageous enough to take and make the game-winning shot? By all accounts, Jordan and James are extraordinarily tough, hardworking, respected, intelligent leaders—as are Durant and Curry. Winners? Tough in the clutch? All four of these GOAT candidates have been, to the highest degree.

Some claim that the NBA was a tougher league in Jordan's day. Scores were low because players worked so hard on defense, and offensive points were difficult to come by. Others claim that today's players are better athletes. While the average height of an NBA player—compared to Jordan's day—remains about 6 feet 7 inches (201 cm), the average weight is 10 pounds (4.5 kg) heavier—and that is 10 pounds of muscle. Players are better shooters today as well. In the 1986–1987 season, NBA players shot .301 from the three-point arc. In 2017–2018, they shot .362 from the arc. So while Jordan played in a tougher, more physical league, James operates against more skilled, athletic players.

Even after analyzing the data, the determination of any sport's GOAT is a matter of subjective opinion. There are countless factors that make up any given player's career, and no matter how advanced the statistics and calculations, there is no definitive answer. In the end, it is up to the fans to decide.

GLOSSARY

All-American A selection as one of the best players in the nation by one of many organizations, such as the Associated Press or *USA Today*.

assist A pass to a player that results in a made field goal by that player.

athleticism The physical qualities associated with an excellent athlete, such as foot speed, quick movements, and agility.

crab walk To walk with one's hands and feet, with the stomach facing upward.

double-team To use two defenders to guard one player (typically a skilled scorer).

duck walk To walk solely on one's feet while crouched low.

field goal Any successful basketball shot that is not a free throw, including two-pointers and three-pointers.

first-team All-American An All-American who is seen as the very best in the country at his or her position.

free agent A player who is no longer under contract with a team and is free to sign with another team.

Hall of Famer In this context, a member of the Naismith Memorial Basketball Hall of Fame.

jump shot A shot made while jumping and releasing the ball at the peak of the jump.

lane The rectangular area that extends from the basket to the free-throw line.

NBA All-Star Game A game played each February featuring the twelve top players from the Western Conference against the twelve best from the Eastern Conference.

NBA draft lottery An event in which the teams that missed the playoffs the previous season participate in a lottery process to determine the draft order in the upcoming NBA draft.

NBA MVP Award The honor given to the league's most valuable player, as selected by a panel of sportswriters and broadcasters who cover NBA teams.

snub To reject.

360 Refers to a 360-degree dunk; the player rotates all the way around while in midair before slamming the ball through the hoop.

unanimous A situation in which everyone is in agreement or makes the same selection.

varsity The top-level team at a high school, college, or university.

FOR MORE INFORMATION

American Mathematical Society (AMS)
201 Charles Street
Providence, RI 02904
(800) 321-4267
Website: https://www.ams.org
Facebook, Instagram, and Twitter: @amermathsoc
The AMS promotes math education for all ages. Its website includes sections dedicated to both learning and applying math outside of an academic setting.

Basketball Reference
6757 Greene Street, Suite 315
Philadelphia, PA 19119
(888) 512-8907
Website: https://www.basketball-reference.com
Facebook and Instagram: @Basketball.Reference
Twitter: @bball_ref
Basketball Reference provides complete statistics on every current and former NBA player and team, including complex stats such as box plus/minus and value over replacement player.

Canada Basketball
1 Westside Drive, Suite 11
Etobicoke, ON M9C 1B2
Canada
(416) 614-8037
Facebook: @CanadaBasketball
Twitter: @CanBball

The governing body of all Canadian basketball, this organization is responsible for spreading the popularity of the sport outside the United States. It also organized international competitions for Canadian basketball players.

Entertainment and Sports Programming Network (ESPN)
ESPN Plaza
Bristol, CT 06010
(888) 549-3776
Website: http://www.espn.com
Facebook, Instagram, and Twitter: @ESPN
A giant in the field of sports journalism, ESPN prides itself on independent, objective reporting.

National Basketball Association (NBA)
545 Fifth Avenue
New York, NY 10017
(844) 622-8550
Website: http://www.NBA.com
Facebook, Instagram, and Twitter: @NBA
The NBA's website features in-depth information on all of its current players, including news and stats.

National Basketball League of Canada (NBLC)
Website: http://www.nblcanada.com
Facebook and Twitter: @NBLCanada
Instagram: @nbl_canada
As the only professional basketball league domestic to Canada, the NBLC oversees an eight-team league that is growing in popularity.

USA Basketball
27 South Tejon Street, Suite 100
Colorado Springs, CO 80903
(719) 590-4800
Website: https://www.usab.com
Facebook, Instagram, and Twitter: @usabasketball
USA Basketball is responsible for the training and fielding of US teams that compete in international tournaments and for the development of young players. The website has a variety of information for potential participants and fans.

FOR FURTHER READING

Anderson, Kirsten. *Who Is Michael Jordan?* New York, NY: Penguin, 2019.

Bradley, Michael. *Stathead Basketball: How Data Changed the Sport*. North Mankato, MN: Compass Point Books, 2019.

Braun, Eric. *Basketball Stats and the Stories Behind Them: What Every Fan Needs to Know*. North Mankato, MN: Capstone Press, 2016.

Christopher, Matt. *Stephen Curry*. Boston, MA: Little, Brown & Co., 2017.

Doeden, Matt. *Fantasy Basketball Math: Using Stats to Score Big in Your League*. Mankato, MN: Capstone Publishers, 2017.

Graubart, Norman. *The Science of Basketball*. New York, NY: Rosen Publishing, 2016.

Mikoley, Kate. *Basketball: Stats, Facts, and Figures*. New York, NY: Gareth Stevens Publishing, 2018.

Mooney, Carla. *Using Math in Sports*. New York, NY: Rosen Publishing, 2018.

Nagelhout, Ryan. *LeBron James: Basketball's King*. New York, NY: Lucent Press, 2017.

Walters, John. *Top 10 Basketball Superstars*. Mankato, MN: The Child's World, 2019.

BIBLIOGRAPHY

Abbott, Henry. "Stephen Curry Isn't Just the MVP—He Is Revolutionizing the Game." ESPN.com, March 18, 2016. http://www.espn.com.

Babcock, Charles. "Secrets of NBA Stephen Curry's Shooting Hidden in Data." InformationWeek, December 29, 2015. https://www.informationweek.com.

Blackmore, Ben. "The Original Dream Team." ESPN.com, January 19, 2012. http://en.espn.co.uk/olympic-sports/sport/story/131630.html.

Brown, Chip. "UT's Durant: Righteous Talent." *Dallas Morning News*, November 8, 2006.

CNN. "Kevin Durant in Tears: Mom Is the 'Real MVP.'" YouTube, May 7, 2014. https://www.youtube.com/watch?v=NmRJgKbibB8.

Cohen, Ben. "Stephen Curry's Science of Sweet Shooting," *Wall Street Journal*, December 17, 2014. https://www.wsj.com/articles/stephen-currys-science-of-sweet-shooting-1418766120.

Friend, Tom. "The Splash Fathers Know Best." ESPN.com, June 2, 2015. http://www.espn.com/nba/playoffs/2015/story/_/id/12819951/splash-fathers-dell-curry-mychal-thompson.

James, LeBron. "I'm Coming Back to Cleveland." *Sports Illustrated*, July 11, 2014. https://www.si.com/nba/2014/07/11/lebron-james-cleveland-cavaliers.

Jenkins, Lee. "LeBron James Chases the Ghost from Chicago and Basketball Immortality," *Sports Illustrated*, August 2, 2016. https://www.si.com.

Jones, Ryan. *King James: Believe the Hype*. New York, NY: St. Martin's Press, 2003.

Limpert, Caroline. "Lessons from Basketball's Olympic 'Dream Team.'" Inc.com, July 11, 2012. https://www.inc.com/olympics/caroline-limpert/how-to-lead-a-team-of-superstars.html.

Maese, Rick. "Kevin Durant, the NBA's Unassuming Superstar, Remembers His D.C. Roots." *Washington Post*, February 24, 2012. https://www.washingtonpost.com.

NBA.com. "Stephen Curry's High School Years." http://www.nba.com/warriors/video/teams/warriors/2015/12/03/1449161678290-curryhighschool120315mp4-150596.

Newsweek Special Edition. "Michael Jordan Didn't Make Varsity—At First." *Newsweek*, October 17, 2015. https://www.newsweek.com/missing-cut-382954.

Parker, Chris. *King James Brings the Land a Crown: The Definitive Tale of the Cavaliers' 2016 Title Run*. N.p.: Mountain Lion Press, 2016.

Ramsey, David. "Thunder's Durant Finds a Different Calling in the NBA." *Deseret News*, April 22, 2011. https://www.deseretnews.com.

Schwartz, Nick. "LeBron Describes the Moment He Felt He Surpassed Michael Jordan as the GOAT." *USA Today*, December 31, 2018. https://ftw.usatoday.com.

INDEX

ABOUT THE AUTHOR

Growing up in Michigan, David Aretha enjoyed math more than any other subject until he discovered the joys of writing. He has authored and edited dozens of sports books, including multiple books on Michael Jordan. For middle school readers, he authored biographies on LeBron James, Kevin Durant, and Stephen Curry. For Topps trading cards, he penned back-of-the-card bios on hundreds of NBA stars.

PHOTO CREDITS

Cover (top left) Harry How/Getty Images, (top right) Jason Miller/Getty Images, (bottom left) Matteo Marchi/Getty Images, (bottom right) Jonathan Daniel/Getty Images; pp. 7, 24 © AP Images; p. 9 Focus on Sport/Getty Images; p. 11 Dimitri Iundt/Corbis Sport/Getty Images; p. 12 Anacleto Rapping/Los Angeles Times/Getty Images; p. 15 John W. McDonough/Sports Illustrated/Getty Images; p. 18 Al Tielemans/Sports Illustrated/ Getty Images; p. 20 Manny Millan/Sports Illustrated/Getty Images; p. 23 Angelo Merendino/Getty Images; p. 27 Andy Lyons/Getty Images; pp. 28, 37 Icon Sportswire/Getty Images; pp. 30, 33, 42 Ezra Shaw/Getty Images; p. 36 Jim Redman/WireImage/Getty Images; p. 41 Mike Stobe/Getty Images; p. 45 Paul Buck/AFP/Getty Images; p. 50 Mike Ehrmann/Getty Images.

Design & Layout: Brian Garvey; Editor: Siyavush Saidian; Photo Researcher: Sherri Jackson